Accounting Terms Dictionary

CW01095636

Accounting Terms Dictionary

Alan J Robb MCom, ACA, CMA, ANZIM
Senior Lecturer in Accountancy
University of Canterbury

and

Roy W Wallis BCom, IPFA, MIIA
Head of the School of Accounting and Finance
Lancashire Polytechnic

Pitman

PITMAN PUBLISHING LIMITED
128 Long Acre, London WC2E 9AN

PITMAN PUBLISHING INC
1020 Plain Street, Marshfield, Massachusetts 02050

Associated Companies
Pitman Publishing Pty Ltd, Melbourne
Pitman Publishing New Zealand Ltd, Wellington
Copp Clark Pitman, Toronto
Original version first published by Whitcoulls Publishers 1981

© Alan J Robb 1981

This adaptation first published in Great Britain 1985 by Pitman Publishing Limited
New and revised material © Pitman Publishing Limited 1985

British Library Cataloguing in Publication Data

    Robb, Alan J.
    Accounting Terms Dictionary. [New ed.]
    1. Accounting–Dictionaries
    I. Title, II. Wallis, Roy W.
    657′.03′21   HF 5621
    ISBN 0–273–02289–X

Printed in Great Britain at The Bath Press, Avon

Preface

This dictionary was originally prepared in 1981 by Alan J Robb of the University of Canterbury at Christchurch, New Zealand, to meet the needs of students of accountancy and business people requiring an understanding of the language of accountants.

Its success led in 1983 to the publication of a revised and expanded version entitled *Australian Dictionary of Accounting Terms*. This new version attempts to meet a similar need in the UK. Its compilation has leant heavily upon the two preceding versions which are aimed at the promotion of a greater and clearer understanding, and consistency in the use, of accounting terms.

The modifications which were necessary were of two main kinds. First, the different legal and institutional framework of the UK necessitated the deletion or amendment of terms or the introduction of new ones. Second, there are some words, phrases or terms which are more commonly used, or by contrast less frequently employed, in business or education circles in Australasia than in the UK. These arise from different degrees of emphasis on what is regarded as important in developments in accounting theory and practice and how it is taught and debated. I have sought to allow for these differing emphases without departing from the rigour or consistency of the earlier versions. In one main respect there is an omission compared with the Australian version. I have not included the more detailed terminology of CoCoA – continuously contemporary accounting – since this would in the UK be of more academic than practical use.

I have sought rather to include the terminology generated as a result of the most recent influences of the Companies Acts and the Accounting Standards Committee.

The resulting version would have been the poorer had it not

Preface

been for the constructive criticism and suggestions made by my colleagues in the School of Accounting and Finance, in particular Henry Lunt, and the invaluable efforts of Margaret Adams and Rita Dickinson. I alone bear the responsibility for any errors of omission or commission.

Roy W Wallis
July 1985

The use of this dictionary

This dictionary will yield maximum benefit if it is kept close at hand and referred to frequently when unfamiliar terms are encountered. In order to achieve conciseness and to avoid undue repetition some explanations necessarily contain other terms found elsewhere in the dictionary. Consequently the user should be prepared to draw on these other terms accordingly to achieve the completeness of understanding he or she requires.

Where some terms are particularly relevant to, or whose importance arises from, Statements of Standard Accounting Practice (SSAPs) or Exposure Drafts (EDs) thereof, promulgated by the Accounting Standards Committee then the relevant standard is inserted and numbered in parentheses after the term thus – (SSAP 16). It should be remembered that these may be subject to change or replacement from time to time as standards evolve or are modified.

The terms explained are *not* legal definitions or necessarily precisely the same as those used in formal statements by professional bodies and those requiring such statements should refer to the appropriate source.

Apart from the obvious use of the dictionary for business people and students generally desiring a knowledge of accounting terminology there are other uses.

First, students who take professional examinations with little, if any, oral tuition will find it useful for revision purposes as a quick reference to, and reminder of, many terms they have encountered in their studies. Second, students who attend lectures can note terms which a lecturer, too often possibly, takes for granted for later clarification. Equally, a lecturer can more readily assume that students having a copy are equipped to follow up points of detail on their own. Finally, the dictionary may be used more positively as a teaching aid by selecting terms for seminar or tutorial discussion as to alternative definitions or as a framework for essay or coursework preparation.

An imaginative tutor will no doubt find further uses.

A

abnormal item   A transaction reported in published financial statements which arises from the ordinary course of business but is by reason of size or effect so exceptional or material that separate disclosure is required.—Contrast extraordinary item (SSAP 6)

abridged accounts   Accounts published in a form less complete than for a company's members or for filing with the Registrar of Companies. Such publications must, *inter alia*, indicate that they are not full accounts.—See full accounts.

absorption costing   Methods of assigning costs with units of production, or service, which assign both costs directly identifiable with product units and those only indirectly related (overheads). Also called full costing.—Contrast direct costing.

ACA   An abbreviation indicating Associate membership of the Institute of Chartered Accountants in England and Wales (ICAEW).

ACCA   The designatory letters for an Associate Member of the Chartered Association of Certified Accountants.

accelerated capital allowances   The deduction allowed against earnings by the Inland Revenue in lieu of depreciation expense whereby until 1984 the whole of the cost of an asset was allowed in the first year of purchase. This allowance is now reduced and ceases in 1986.—See depreciation.

accelerated depreciation   See accelerated capital allowances.

acceptance of bill of exchange   Acceptance of a bill of exchange is the act by which the obligation becomes binding on the drawee (the party which is obligated to make payment under the bill). The drawee indicates his acceptance of a bill by signing the face of the bill, at which time the drawee becomes known as the acceptor.

1

account   A record in an accounting system for accumulating chronologically additions, deductions and balances of individual assets, liabilities, owners' equity, revenues or expenses.

account form (or format)   The form of presentation for the two main financial statements viz. the profit and loss account and balance sheet, which represents the traditional debit/credit or left hand/right hand layout of accounts in the ledger. Also called 'T' form or horizontal format.—Contrast narrative form or vertical format.

accountancy   The body of knowledge and skills pertaining to the accounting process and/or the application thereof in practice. The terms accountancy and accounting are often used synonymously.

accountant   One who practises accountancy, especially one who is qualified by membership of a recognised professional body.

accounting   The process of identifying, measuring, and communicating economic information about an entity to permit informed judgments and decisions by users of the information.

accounting bases   The methods, principles or rules available for measuring and recording transactions of different types. Alternative bases may exist e.g. different methods of stock valuation (SSAP 2).—See accounting policies.

accounting cycle   The sequence of accounting procedures for processing transactions during the accounting year:
  (a) collecting transaction data
  (b) analysing and recording in journals or other prime entry records
  (c) posting to appropriate ledger accounts
  (d) balancing ledger accounts and preparing end-of-period trial balance
  (e) making period-end adjustments
  (f) preparing second trial balance from amended ledger accounts
  (g) making closing journal entries
  (h) preparing financial statements

(i) reversing any necessary entries as at the start of the next accounting period.

Initially (e), (f) and (h) may be performed or prepared using a worksheet prior to the formal entries being made in the accounting records. Some of these stages may be unnecessary.

accounting entity See entity.

accounting equation The statement that the equities of an entity equal its assets at any given time. This statement is the basis of double-entry accounting and is expressed as:

$A = L + OE$ where A is assets
L is liabilities
OE is owners' equity.

The expanded and dynamic form of the equation for a period is:

$A + \Delta A = L + \Delta L + [OE + \Delta OE + (R - E)]$

where in relation to the period:

A   is assets at the start
ΔA is the change in assets
L   is liabilities at the start
ΔL is the change in liabilities
OE   is owners' equity at the start
ΔOE is the change in owners' equity other than by way of revenue and expenses
R   is revenues for the period
E   is expenses for the period

Also called the double-entry equation.

accounting manual(s) A set of instructions as to the organisation, procedures and methods to be followed in establishing and/or operating an accounting system.

accounting period The selected time period for which financial reports are prepared, normally one year.—See financial statements, interim reports.

accounting policies The accounting bases actually adopted and declared by an entity. (SSAP 2)

account sales A statement rendered by one party to another detailing particulars of sales made on the other's behalf and net amounts owing. Account sales are used, for example, by consignees in accounting to consignors or by publishers when making royalty payments to authors.

accounts payable   Current liabilities representing amounts owed by an entity, normally as the result of the purchase of goods or services. Also called creditors, sundry creditors, trade creditors.

accounts receivable   Current assets representing amounts owed to an entity normally as the result of the sale of goods or services. Also called debtors, sundry debtors, receivables, trade debtors.

accretion   The increase in economic worth of an asset through physical change, rather than through market forces. The physical change may arise from either natural growth or an aging process, e.g. timber.—Contrast appreciation, depreciation.

accrual   See accrual accounting.

accrual accounting   The method of accounting for the revenues and expenses of a period as they are earned or incurred, regardless of the time when cash is received or paid.—Contrast cash accounting.

accrual(s) basis (or concept)   The principle that the actual cash receipts or payments recorded *in* an accounting period should be adjusted where required to ensure the revenues and expenses *of* the period are reported regardless of when the associated cash flows occur.

accrued expense(s)   Expense(s) relating to an accounting period but not recorded by the end of the period, thus requiring an adjustment to any (smaller) amount recorded.—Compare accrued revenue(s).

accrued revenue(s)   Revenue(s) relating to an accounting period unrecorded by the end of the period requiring insertion.—Compare accrued expense(s).

accumulated depreciation   The amount recorded as the total reduction of the value of an asset since acquisition due to depreciation.

accumulated funds   The members' interest in a not-for-profit organisation such as a club. Alternatively, the recorded total of amounts accumulated for a specific or general purpose.

acid test   A test of how liquid an entity is by reference to its ratio of liquid assets to current liabilities.—See quick ratio.

ACMA   Abbreviation indicating Associate membership of the Institute of Cost and Management Accountants.

acquisition cost   The net invoice price of an asset or service together with all expenditures incurred in placing and preparing that asset or service for its intended use. Such expenditures include legal fees, freight in, customs duty, and installation costs. Also called historical price, original cost, outlay cost.

adjusting events   Post-balance sheet events which require alterations to be made to the financial statements of the period just ended before publication because they materially affect the items therein (SSAP 17).

adjusting entries (or adjustments)   See period-end adjustments.

administration expenses   The expenses related to the enterprise as a whole as distinct from the expenses which are related to specific functions such as manufacturing, selling and distribution, or financial.

AICPA   An abbreviation indicating membership of the American Institute of Certified Public Accountants.

allocate   To apportion, assign or spread a cost or revenue to more than one account, product, service, activity, department, period etc. Various bases of allocation are used.

allotment of shares   The allocation of shares in a company by the directors following an application or offer to take up the shares. Decisions as to the persons to whom shares are allotted, and the number allotted to each, are at the absolute discretion of the directors. If an issue of shares is over-subscribed, i.e. the number of shares applied for exceeds the number available for issue, the excess must be eliminated either by rejecting some applications altogether, or by reducing the number of shares allotted to some or all of the applicants.

allotment letter   A letter sent to each successful applicant to an issue of shares advising the number of shares the directors have allotted to the applicant. A letter of regret, together with a refund of application money, is sent to those whose applications have been refused.

allotted capital   See issued capital.

American Institute of Certified Public Accountants   The organisation of certified public accountants in the USA.

amortisation   The writing off of an asset's recorded value over the accounting periods assumed to have benefited from its use. The term is usually used in connection with intangible assets.—See depreciation.

annual accounts   The year end financial statements, especially income statement and balance sheet, of an entity. Often required by law and accompanied by an annual report on the entity's activities.

application for shares   An offer to subscribe to a new issue of shares to be made by a public company. The applicant generally completes an application form enclosed with the prospectus and forwards this with a deposit, known as application money, to the issuing company. The application is not a completed contract, only an offer to subscribe for shares.

application of funds   Any transaction that reduces the funds available to an entity e.g. by purchasing an asset or repaying a liability. Also called disposition or use of funds.

applied overhead   Overhead costs allocated to departments, products or activities. Normally overhead costs are applied using predetermined rates based on budgeted costs for a period.

appraisal   The process of valuing an asset or liability other than by an explicit market transaction.—See investment appraisal.

appreciation   The increase in economic worth of an asset caused by market forces rather than physical change.—Contrast accretion, diminution.

appropriation account   See profit and loss appropriation account.

appropriation of profits   The segregation or restriction of a portion of retained earnings (balance of profit and loss appropriation account) for a particular purpose e.g. to provide for a proposed dividend.

approval, sale on   A transaction where goods are supplied to a customer who has the option of either returning them if they are unacceptable, or retaining them for use. If the goods are retained, a sale is deemed to have taken place. Also called sale on appro.

articles of association   The internal regulations of a company which describe in some detail the manner in which the company's business shall be conducted. It is one of two main documents, the other being the memorandum of association, which must be filed with the Registrar of Companies upon the formation of a company. The articles will usually specify rules for the making of calls, the transfer of shares, the declaration and basis for dividends, the capitalisation of profits, the forfeiture of shares and other matters affecting the shareholders and the company. If the articles are silent on any point the articles in Table A of the Companies Act 1985 are deemed to apply.

asset cover   The extent to which borrowings can be met or covered by available assets as shown by their book value.

asset register   A record containing details of each significant fixed asset or group of assets held by an entity. The details will include a description of the assets and their location, the original costs or valuations, the depreciation written off to date, the estimated economic lives, and the estimated residual values.

asset(s)   An asset is something of worth to an entity, having a capacity to provide future economic benefits, and which is owned or controlled as a result of a past transaction or event. The essential characteristics of an asset are:

(a) it must provide future benefits involving a contribution to the entity's future positive net cash flows
(b) it must benefit the entity which has the use of it, and
(c) the entity must have a legally enforceable claim to the benefits arising

—See current assets, fixed assets, fungible assets, intangible assets.

assignment, assignor, assignee   An absolute transfer by deed of some right, interest, property or goods by one person (the assignor) to another (the assignee).

associated company   A company in which another (the investing company):

(a) holds and intends to retain as a long term investment, a substantial equity interest, and
(b) is in a position to exercise significant influence over its financial and operating policies.

   In the absence of evidence to the contrary there is a presumption that a holding of 20 per cent or more of the equity voting rights is a substantial equity interest.

   Representation on the associated company's board of directors will usually be taken as indicating a position to exercise significant influence. (SSAP 1)—Compare subsidiary company.

attestation   The act of bearing witness to the fact that a signature has been appended to a document. The attestation function of auditing is the expressing of an opinion as to the truth and fairness of financial statements.

audit

(a) Noun – A systematic examination of financial statements and the accounts and data from which they have been compiled, by an independent party with the objective of expressing an opinion as to the accuracy, truth and fairness with which the financial statements present the financial position and results of the entity concerned. The auditor's

opinion is usually conveyed in the form of an audit report
to those recipients of the financial statements for whose
benefit he is appointed e.g. the shareholders of a
company.—Compare internal audit.
(b) Verb – The process of conducting such an examination.

auditor   A person appointed to conduct an audit, whose
qualification to act as auditor may be prescribed by law in the
case of some entities e.g. companies.

authorised capital   The amount of share capital which a
company is permitted to issue. Also called nominal capital.—
See issued capital, uncalled capital, paid-up capital.

avoidable costs   Costs that may be saved by not adopting a
given alternative.—See incremental cost, variable costs.—
Compare controllable costs.

avoidance of tax   The minimisation of the liability for taxation
by the appropriate arrangement of affairs, while fulfilling all
statutory requirements.—Contrast evasion of tax.

B

bad debts   Uncollectable accounts receivable. They represent losses which should be written off immediately.—Compare doubtful debts.

bad debts recovered   The collection, in whole or in part, of specific accounts receivable previously written off as uncollectable.

balance
  (a) Noun – the difference between the debit and credit entries in an account at a point in time thus showing the net effect on the entity of the type of transaction recorded in the account to date.
  (b) Verb – the ascertainment of the balance on an account, or for all accounts, by netting the debit and credit entries.

balance date (day) adjustments   See period-end adjustments.

balance sheet   A statement of assets, liabilities and owners' equity at a specific date. Also called statement of financial position, statement of assets and liabilities.—See account form.

bank overdraft   The amount by which a bank allows a customer to overdraw or go into its debt.

bank reconciliation   A procedure or schedule which explains how any difference between the entity's ledger balance of the bank account and the balance in the statement issued by the bank arose. The difference is made up of such items as outstanding bankings, unpresented cheques, bank charges and errors.

banking(s)   Amount(s) paid into a bank.—See lodgement(s)

bankruptcy   See insolvency.

bear   One who believes that security prices will fall and sells hoping to buy back at a lower price. A 'bear' market is one in which share prices are generally declining.—Contrast bull.

bill of exchange   An unconditional order in writing given by one person to another, signed by the person giving it, requiring the person to whom it is addressed to pay on demand or at a fixed or determinable future time a sum certain in money to or to the order of a specified person or to bearer. A bill of exchange thus originates with the party that is requiring payment (the drawer) and becomes binding on the party whom it is intended to make ultimately liable (the drawee) as soon as he has agreed by acceptance, which is effected by signature across the face of the bill. The drawee then becomes known as the acceptor. Bills of exchange are frequently used to settle foreign transactions involving the shipment of goods between countries.—Compare promissory notes.

bill of lading   A document issued by a shipping company representing title to goods being shipped.—Contrast consignment note, way-bill.

bill payable   A liability of an entity arising either as a result of giving a promissory note or accepting a bill of exchange drawn on it by a creditor.

bill receivable   An asset of an entity arising either as a result of receiving a promissory note or drawing a bill of exchange on a debtor.

board of directors   The governing body of a company elected by the shareholders at the annual general meeting.

bond   A formal evidence of a debt, issued by a company, public corporation or Government, whereby the borrower promises to pay the lender a specified amount at a specified time with interest at a fixed rate payable on specified dates. It is similar to a debenture.

Goods held in 'bond' are those on which customs or other duty has not yet been paid.

bonus   A payment over and above the normal wage or salary paid to an employee usually for meritorious performance or as a consequence of the entity having had a successful year.

bonus dividend   An abnormal dividend declared out of profits. If paid in cash it is regarded as an increment to the normal dividend and is unlikely to be repeated in future periods e.g. an additional dividend paid in the centenary year of a company. Instead of being paid in cash, the bonus dividend may be applied to the payment, in full or in part, of amounts owing on a new share issue. The dividend may also be applied to the payment of any uncalled capital on shares which have already been issued.—See bonus issue.

bonus issue   An issue of shares to existing shareholders through the capitalisation of profits and for which no payment is required. The term can be applied to the capitalisation of profits for either a new issue of fully or partly paid up shares, or the cancelling of uncalled capital on existing issued shares. Also called a scrip issue.—See bonus dividend.

book-keeping   The process of recording transactions in an accounting system, nowadays including computerised systems.

book value   The net amount shown in the books or in the accounts for any asset, liability or owners' equity item. In the case of a fixed asset it is equal to the recorded cost or valuation of the asset less accumulated depreciation. The book value of a firm is its net assets, i.e. the excess of total assets over total liabilities.

branch account(s)   Records kept to identify the financial results of a branch or part of an organisation. Branch accounts may be kept separately by the branch, or by the head office as part of its own accounts.

breakeven point   The point at which revenues earned equal the fixed and variable costs incurred in producing and selling the output concerned, and at which neither profit nor loss is made.

brokerage   A commission charged by an agent or dealer (broker) for services rendered e.g. in underwriting a share issue.

budget   A schedule, document or statement giving a quantitative expression of a proposed plan of action as an aid to its co-ordination and implementation. Budgets are prepared mainly for sales, production, revenue, expense, capital expenditure and cash, and can be summarised in a forecasted balance sheet and profit and loss account. It is frequently used to help control operations and to evaluate performance.

budget centre A department or part of an entity for which a budget is drawn up.

bull One who believes that security prices will rise and buys to sell later at a profit. A 'bull' market is one in which share prices are generally rising.—Contrast bear.

C

CA   Abbreviation indicating membership of the ICAS.

called up   A term relating to the total amount due from shareholders etc. who are subscribing capital by instalments. Part of this total may already have been paid.—Contrast uncalled capital.

capital   A term used to describe the owner's equity or proprietorship in a business. Capital is a stock of wealth that can provide future services and should be contrasted with income which is a flow of wealth or services in excess of that necessary to maintain a given level of capital.

capital asset   An asset intended to remain in the entity on a permanent or long-term basis to provide continuing economic benefits e.g. land, plant.—See fixed asset.

capital employed   The funds available to an entity to carry on its activities. More specifically those funds provided by the owners on starting up or accumulated out of profits or surpluses.

capital expenditure   Expenditure which is expected to produce benefits in periods beyond that in which the expenditure is incurred, and is treated as an asset.—Contrast revenue expenditure.

capital gain   An increase in the value of an asset over its original cost, especially when realised by sale.

capital loss   A decrease in value of an asset, beyond that occurring through depreciation, below its original cost.

capital reserve   A reserve which is regarded as not being available for distribution as a dividend through the profit and loss account for statutory reasons or because of the requirements of the memorandum or articles of association of a company or because of a resolution of the directors.—Contrast revenue reserve.—See reserve.

capital transaction   Transaction affecting the financial position of an entity beyond the period in which the transaction takes place e.g. capital expenditure, raising a loan (long-term).

capitalisation issue   See bonus issue, scrip issue.

capitalise   To record an expenditure as an asset rather than an expense, or to transfer amounts of revenue reserves or retained earnings to capital or other non-distributable accounts.

carriage in   The delivery cost incurred in acquiring goods or assets. It is treated as an expense unless capitalised as part of the cost of a fixed asset.

carriage out   A seller's delivery cost, treated either as a general selling expense or a cost of disposal of a fixed asset.

carrying cost   The cost of holding or storing inventory from the time of purchase until the time of sale.

cash   Currency, coins, cheques, and balances in bank accounts—a current asset.

cash accounting   The method of accounting for the revenue and expenses of a period as they are received or paid in cash.—Contrast accrual accounting; cash-flow accounting.

cash book   A combination of a cash payments journal and a cash receipts journal to form a ledger account in which a running balance of the cash on hand and at bank is recorded. May be kept separately from the main ledger.

cash budget   A schedule of expected cash receipts and disbursements for a period. The cash inflows and outflows in the cash budget are those that should result from the plans embodied in the other budgets normally prepared, e.g. sales budget, production budget, expense budget, capital expenditure budget.—Compare cash accounting; cash flow statement.

cash cycle   The period of time during which cash is converted into inventories, inventories are converted into accounts receivable through sales, and receivables are converted back into cash. Also called the earnings cycle.

cash disbursements journal   See cash payments journal.

cash discount   An amount deducted from a debt if payment is made by a particular date or within a specified period after the sale has been invoiced. Cash discount allowed is sometimes called sales discount; cash discount received is sometimes called purchases discount. Contrast trade discount.

cash flow   The total cash receipts (inflow) or payments (outflow) arising from a given asset, or group of assets, for a given period. Net cash flow is the inflows less the outflows.

cash-flow accounting   A method of accounting whose purpose is to produce financial reports which highlight the effect of business operations and decisions on the supply of cash and its utilisation. It seeks to exclude arbitrary allocations of cost or revenue between different periods e.g. for depreciation, which it is argued tend to distract attention from important cash management problems. Sometimes used as a synonym for cash accounting, though the concepts are not identical.— Contrast accrual accounting, cash accounting, net realisable value accounting.

cash-flow statement   A statement summarising the actual flows of cash for a period. A statement of estimated cash flows is a cash budget.—Compare statement of sources and application of funds.

cash payments journal   A journal used to record expenditures by cash or by cheque and direct charges/payments made by the bank. Also called a cash disbursements journal.

cash receipts journal   A journal used to record receipts of cash or cheques and direct lodgements to the bank.

cash value (of life insurance policy)   See surrender value.

C.C.A.   An abbreviation for current cost accounting.

CCAB   Abbreviation for the Consultative Committee of Accountancy Bodies which comprises representatives of the major accountancy bodies in the UK in order to develop and promote a corporate view on matters of common concern.

C.C.E.   See current cash equivalent.

certified public accountant (CPA)   In the United States an accountant who has satisfied the statutory and administrative requirements of his or her jurisdiction to be registered or licensed as a public accountant.

charge   (Noun) – A right of a creditor in some asset so as to recover his debt e.g. by requiring the asset to be sold.
(Verb)– see expense.

charge off   See expense.

chart of accounts   A systematic listing of the titles and references of all accounts found in a ledger.

chartered accountant   A member of a body of accountants empowered by Royal Charter to regulate their professional activities. More specifically the term relates to members of the Institutes of (i) Chartered Accountants of England and Wales (ICAEW), (ii) Chartered Accountants in Ireland (ICAI), and (iii) Chartered Accountants of Scotland (ICAS). It also relates to members of similar bodies in Commonwealth countries. Members of other chartered bodies may not describe themselves as chartered accountants.

cheque   A bill of exchange drawn on a banker and payable on demand.

c.i.f. (cost, insurance, freight)   A term used in contracts and on invoices along with the name of a given port to indicate that the quoted price includes insurance, handling and freight charges up to delivery by the seller at the given port.—Contrast f.o.b. (free on board).

CIPFA   Abbreviation of the Chartered Institute of Public Finance and Accountancy.

circulating capital   A term which has been used in some legal decisions to describe those assets which are used and converted into other assets in the normal activities of the entity during the business cycle. In this sense circulating capital is the current assets of an entity.—Compare circulating monetary assets; working capital.

circulating monetary assets   Monetary assets held by an entity in order to service its day-to-day operations.

closing entries   The entries that transfer balances of nominal accounts to the profit and loss account, and transfer the net profit or net loss to owners' equity.

closing stock   The stock, or inventory, on hand at the end of an accounting period.

COCOA   An abbreviation for continuously contemporary accounting. Usually written CoCoA.

c.o.d. (cash on delivery)   A term used in contracts and on invoices to indicate that the buyer must pay for the goods at the time of delivery.

collateral   Assets that are pledged by a borrower and that will be forfeited if the loan is not repaid in accordance with stipulated conditions, especially as to the date that repayment is due.

common dollar accounting   See current purchasing power accounting.

common stock   North American term for ordinary shares.

company   An entity which is legally incorporated and whose membership and governance must comply with the requirements of the Companies Act. Different types are possible–see limited liability company.

compound journal entry   A journal entry with more than one debit and/or more than one credit.

comptroller   See controller.

conservatism   An accounting procedure requiring that judgmental determinations should tend towards understatement rather than overstatement of assets and income. Conservatism results in the recognition of expenses and of all losses, whether realised or unrealised, but defers recognition of gains or profits until they are realised. Also called prudence. (SSAP 2).

consignee, consignor   See consignment.

consignment   The act of delivering goods; also the goods themselves so delivered. Goods are said to be 'on consignment' if they are delivered by the owner (the consignor) to another (the consignee) to be sold by the consignee on behalf of the consignor. The consignee usually receives a commission for his part in selling the goods. The goods are the property of the consignor until sold.

consignment note   A document describing goods to be delivered and giving instructions to a carrier for their delivery.—Contrast bill of lading, way-bill.

consistency   The use of the same accounting practices by an entity both within a period and from period to period. Consistency does not preclude changes in practices where there is adequate reason for change.—Contrast uniformity. (SSAP 2)

consolidated financial statements   Statements issued by legally separate but related companies that show financial position and income as they would appear if the companies were one legal entity. Such statements reflect an economic rather than a legal concept of the entity. The Companies Act 1948 requires a company with subsidiaries to present to its shareholders group accounts, normally in the form of consolidated financial statements, when its own balance sheet is presented.— Compare associated company; parent company; subsidiary company. (SSAP 14)

constant money value concept   See stable monetary unit assumption.

contingency   A condition or situation, which exists at balance date, the ultimate outcome of which, gain or loss, is uncertain and will be confirmed only on the occurrence or non-occurrence, of one or more future events after the date of approval of the financial statements. A contingency may or may not give rise to an asset or a liability. The treatment of a contingent asset or liability will vary from inclusion within the financial statements, if there is a high probability of subsequent events confirming the existence of the asset or liability, to inclusion by way of a note where the probability of confirmation is remote. (SSAP 18)

contingent liability   See contingency.

continuity of operations   See going concern.

continuously contemporary accounting (CoCoA)   A system of accounting which has been advocated based upon continually updating records to reflect the market resale prices of assets. It is intended to adapt accounting data to counter relative price changes.

contra   An entry made either between accounts or within the same account which is intended to make transfers, adjustments or cancellations to existing data rather than record new transactions e.g. where a customer's debt is offset against the entity's debt to him to allow for a net payment.

contra account   An account that accumulates data and which is subtracted from another account in financial statements. For example, accumulated depreciation on plant and equipment.

contribution margin   The excess of revenue over variable costs for an identifiable activity. The contribution margin per unit is the amount, represented by the per unit selling price less variable costs, which each unit is assumed to contribute towards the absorption of fixed costs and producing a profit.

control account   An account in the general ledger the balance of which reflects the aggregate balances of a number of related subsidiary ledger accounts and thus summarises or controls these records.

controllable costs   Those costs that may be directly influenced at a particular level of responsibility within a given time span. Controllable costs may be either variable or fixed.—Compare avoidable costs.

controller   A title often used, especially in North America, for the chief accountant of an organisation. Also called comptroller.

corporation   A legally incorporated entity especially in the US. In UK now often used as synonym for company but usually to indicate public sector bodies e.g. BBC.

corporation tax   A tax levied on the profits or income of a legally incorporated entity in contrast to an individual.—See income tax.

cost   The sacrifice made, measured by the price paid or required to be paid, to acquire goods, services or other future economic benefits.—Compare expense; loss.—Contrast value.

cost accounting   That part of management accounting concerned with recording and allocating costs. Often taken to include the establishment of cost budgets and reporting actual cost variances therefrom.

cost centre   The area of responsibility, location, function or unit of activity for which costs are accumulated.

cost of capital   The amount which an entity effectively must pay for its capital funds. The calculation may relate to specific types of finance, or to capital employed defined in different ways, and may be a weighted average to reflect proportions of different types of finance (WACC).

cost of goods manufactured   The sum of all costs charged or allocated to products whose manufacture is completed during a period.—Contrast cost of goods sold.

cost of goods sold   The cost of inventory sold during a period; an expense in the end of period financial statements. Equals beginning inventory plus purchases and/or cost of goods manufactured minus ending inventory. It may be calculated and recorded as sales are made or it may be calculated in the end of period financial statements. Also called cost of sales.

cost of sales   See cost of goods sold.

cover   The extent to which earnings are available to pay shareholders or other investors their normal dividend or interest.

C.P.P.   See current purchasing power accounting.

credit
  (a) An entry signifying an increase in a liability, revenue or owner's equity account or a decrease in an asset or expense account.—Contrast debit.
  (b) A facility extended by a vendor permitting another person (the debtor) to purchase goods or services without making immediate payment.

credit note   A document recording an allowance made for the return of goods previously supplied or to correct an overcharge on the original invoice.

creditors   See accounts payable.

cum div   An indication that a share price includes the right to dividends declared but not yet paid by a company.—Contrast ex div.

cumulative preference dividends   Dividends on preference shares that accrue as a commitment of the company if they are not paid in any year. Arrears of cumulative preference dividends must be paid before any dividends are paid to ordinary shareholders. Unless specifically stated to be non-cumulative, dividends on all preference shares are deemed to be cumulative.

current account   A term used to describe an account in which day-to-day transactions between one party and another party are recorded, e.g. a customer's cheque account with a bank. Where the capital contributions of partners to a partnership are fixed in amount there will usually be also a current account for each partner to record his other transactions with the partnership.

current assets   Cash and other assets that are expected to be converted into cash or to be used in the production of other current assets. The conversion or consumption is expected to occur within one year or the normal operating cycle of the entity whichever is the longer. The term includes prepayments, stock, work-in-process and debtors.

current cash equivalent   The amount of cash for which goods and services can be exchanged.

current cost   A cost stated in terms of a present price rather than in terms of the original or acquisition price.

current cost accounting (CCA)   A system of accounting which reflects the value to the business of goods and services in terms of their replacement cost, economic value or net realisable value, and in which adjustments are made to the income figure to reflect the impact of specific price level changes.—Contrast continuously contemporary accounting; cost accounting. (SSAP 16)

current liabilities   Obligations or debts due to be discharged on demand or within one year.

current purchasing power accounting (C.P.P.)   A system of accounting which reflects the changes in the purchasing power of money in a given period. Also called adjusted historical cost accounting, common dollar accounting, general price level accounting, stabilised accounting.

current ratio   The relationship between current assets and current liabilities, used as a guide in evaluating the solvency of an entity.

current replacement cost   The present cost of replacing an asset with an identical asset or one of equivalent operating capability either by production or by purchase.

customs duty   The duty levied upon goods imported.—Contrast excise duty, sales tax.

D

---

debenture A formal acknowledgment of indebtedness by a company in terms of which the amount borrowed by or deposited with the company will be repaid on an agreed date or under certain conditions. Until repayment, interest is paid on the debenture at defined intervals. A loan or deposit may only be described as a debenture if it is secured over assets of the company. Debentures may be issued at par, at a discount, or at premium. The price of a debenture is frequently quoted as a proportion of 100, e.g. a price 2 per cent below par is '98'.

debit An entry signifying an increase in an asset or expense account or a decrease in a liability, revenue or owner's equity account.—Contrast credit.

debt finance Funds borrowed from outside parties rather than capital supplied by the owners of an entity.—Contrast equity finance.

debtors See accounts receivable.

defalcation The misappropriation or embezzlement of property belonging to another.

default The failure to fulfil an obligation when required; for example, default in payment occurs when principal or interest is not paid on the due date.

deferred charge Expenditure not recognised as an expense of the period when incurred but carried forward to a future period for the purpose of matching against subsequent revenues. Also called deferred asset, deferred cost, deferred expenditure.

deferred cost See deferred charge.

deferred expenditure See deferred charge.

deferred liability   A liability of indeterminate term introduced into the accounting records in order to match revenues and expenses of the current period, e.g. a deferred income tax liability relates to the proportion of income tax expense arising from timing differences in a period.

depletion   The allocation of the cost of a wasting asset or natural resource normally based on its physical exhaustion.—Compare amortisation; depreciation.

depreciable cost   That part of the acquisition cost of an asset less residual value that is to be written off as an expense over the economic life of the asset as depreciation.

depreciable life   The economic life of an asset over which depreciation is calculated.

depreciation   The allocation as an expense of the cost or value of an asset, less the net amount expected to be recovered on disposal of that asset, among a series of accounting periods. The depreciation expense for a period is usually based on: (i) the likely economic life of the asset, (ii) the pattern of reduction in services during its life, and (iii) its likely residual (or salvage) value on disposal at the end of its life.—See accumulated depreciation.—Compare amortisation; depletion.—Contrast accretion. (SSAP 12).

deprival value   The value which an entity would lose if it were deprived of an asset. Conceptually different measures of this value are possible but in practice SSAPs restrict the choice of measure adopted.

direct costing   A method of assigning only variable manufacturing costs to the units produced or other output. Fixed costs are excluded from the unit cost under this method and are classified as period costs as incurred. Also called marginal costing, variable costing.—Contrast absorption costing.

direct costs   Costs which are wholly and exclusively identifiable with whatever is being costed whether a cost centre or cost unit. Some writers use the term to mean variable costs in relation to cost units.

directive(s)   Laws of the European Economic Council requiring member countries to subscribe to common codes of conduct, usually implemented through a member's own laws e.g. Companies Acts 1980, 1981.

disbursement   A payment by cash or cheque. Also called remittance.

disclosure   The displaying or reporting of information in financial statements, reports, notes thereto, or the auditor's report. The Companies Acts require disclosure of some specific items while the various statements of standard accounting practice indicate additional items that should be disclosed. In particular SSAP 2 requires disclosure of the various accounting policies adopted in preparing or presenting financial statements.

discount
(a) The reduction in price granted for prompt payment (cash discount), or for custom (trade discount), or for bulk (quantity discount).
(b) The difference between the face or future value and the present value of a payment.
(c) The amount by which the nominal or par value of stocks, shares or debentures exceeds the price paid to the company at the time of issue.

discount period   The period after a sale during which payment entitles the buyer to deduct any cash discount offered.

discounted value   See present value.

disposition of funds   See application of funds.

dissolution (of a company)   The process by which a company, after winding up, is dissolved by the Registrar of Companies and formally ceases to exist.

distributable income   The portion of net income that can be distributed to owners (usually in the form of dividends) without impairing the operating capability of the firm.— Contrast retained earnings.—See Companies Act 1985.

dividend The distribution of profits recommended by the directors of a company to its shareholders, usually paid in cash and declared at a given rate per cent of a share's nominal value or number of pence per share.—See bonus dividend; bonus issue; liquidation dividend.

dividend yield The relationship between the dividend and the market price of a share. It is usually calculated as the latest total dividend declared for the year divided by market price of the share at a given time. The yield is usually expressed as a percentage.

dividends in arrears Dividends on cumulative preference shares that have not been declared each period in accordance with the terms of their issue.—See cumulative preference dividends.

double entry The system of recording transactions in terms of the accounting equation, such that an equality of debits and credits results.

double-entry equation See accounting equation.

doubtful debts Debts on which it is considered that a loss will be incurred through payment not being received in full. The expected loss might relate to a specific debt but usually will be a proportion of total debts outstanding which from experience it is known will not be collected. Doubtful debts are incorporated into the accounting system by means of a provision as a period-end adjustment. — Contrast bad debts.

draft A bill of exchange. When purchased from a bank in order to settle an international transaction, the bill is drawn by the bank on itself or on a bank in another country. If used to pay for goods, the documents giving title to the goods are frequently attached to the bill which is then sent to the purchaser's bank. The documents are delivered to the purchaser only when he accepts the bill or settles the account by payment.

drawings Economic benefits received by a sole proprietor or partner from the entity during a period. The benefits may be

drawings

cash withdrawn or payments made on behalf of the proprietor/partner or goods taken for personal use. Drawings are not an expense of the entity but are a direct deduction from proprietorship or owner's equity.

E

E. & O.E.   Errors and omissions excepted. This is often placed on a document in order to indicate that the preparer of the document reserves the right to amend the statement should any errors afterwards be discovered.

earnings   Income or profit of an entity. May refer to gross revenues alone or to the net figure after deducting associated expenses.

earnings cycle   The stages in the operations of an entity which give rise to earnings or income. In a manufacturing or retail entity the main stages are:
(a) the acquisition of goods or materials;
(b) the conversion of materials if required, by manufacture;
(c) the sale of finished goods on credit or for cash;
(d) the return to a position so that goods or materials can again be acquired, e.g. by collection of accounts receivable.
Also called operating cycle.—Compare cash cycle.

earnings per share (E.P.S.)   The relationship between earnings and the number of shares issued by a company. It is calculated as net income available to shareholders divided by the weighted average number of shares on issue during a period. It is usually calculated only for ordinary shares (SSAP 3).

earnings yield   The relationship between the earnings per share and the market price of a share. It is calculated as the earnings per share divided by the market price of the share at a given time. The yield is usually expressed as a percentage.

E.B.I.T.   Earnings before interest and tax.

economic life   The time span over which the benefits of an asset are expected to be received. The economic life of an asset is the shortest of its physical, technical, commercial and legal lives (SSAP 12).

elements of cost   The three main categories into which all costs may be divided *viz*. labour, materials and other costs.

endorsement   See indorsement.

entity   A person, partnership, company, or other organisation for which financial statements are prepared. An accounting entity need not be the same as the entity defined by law, e.g. the business of an individual is an accounting entity, but the legal entity of an individual includes both business and personal affairs.

entry value   A value attached to an asset as a result of it 'entering' the entity e.g. its purchase price or valuation—Contrast exit value.

E.P.S.   See earnings per share.

equities
  (a) The total interests of parties in the assets of an entity. Lenders and creditors have a 'specific equity', owners have a 'residual equity'.—Compare debt finance; equity finance.
  (b) In its singular form the proprietor's or shareholders' claim to the net assets of an entity.

equity   See equities.

equity capital employed   The proprietors' capital funds subscribed or retained in the business from profits.—See equity finance.

equity finance   Share capital, retained earnings and reserves of a company.

equity method of accounting   Describes the practice by which an investing company records in its accounts and, where appropriate in a consolidated balance sheet, its investment in an associate company at its cost plus its proportionate share of post-acquisition retained profits and reserves, less any amounts written off.

evasion of tax   An illegal act or omission designed to escape a legitimate liability for taxation, e.g. furnishing false amounts in a return of income.—Contrast avoidance of tax.

excise duty   The duty levied upon goods which are produced or manufactured within a country, e.g. the duty on beer.— Contrast customs duty; sales tax.

exit value   A value attached to an asset as a result of selling or disposing of it. Different measures of exit values are possible. See net realisable value, liquidation value—Contrast entry value.

expenditure   Strictly, the payment or payments of cash to acquire an asset, service or other benefit. In a wider sense the term includes the incurring of a liability for which payment will be made later.

expense
   (a) Noun. The sacrifice involved, as measured in money terms, by payments made or debts incurred for services, or amount(s) of assets used up, in carrying on business in the accounting period concerned.
   (b) Verb. The recording of the particular expense involved arising from expenditure on labour, materials, services or the using up of an asset.

expense account   An account recording a particular expense which is closed at the end of the accounting period by transfer to the profit and loss account. Also used to refer to an allowance to an employee who incurs an expense on behalf of the entity, e.g. entertainment of customers.

expenses prepaid   The amount of expenditures in one accounting period which relates to the next or a future period because of payment in advance. Such amount must be carried forward as an item on the balance sheet—See prepayments.

exposure draft   A proposed statement of standard accounting practice which has been circulated for comment prior to its promulgation by the ASC.

extraordinary items   Items derived from events or transactions that are distinct from the ordinary activities of the business and which are not expected to recur frequently or regularly. They are shown separately after the operating profit in the profit and loss account (SSAP 6).

F

factory cost   See manufacturing cost.

factory overhead   Manufacturing costs other than direct labour, direct materials, or direct expenses.

FCA   The designatory letters for a Fellow of the ICAEW.

FCCA   The designatory letters for a Fellow of the Chartered Association of Certified Accountants.

FCMA   The designatory letters for a Fellow of the ICMA.

fee simple   Land in absolute ownership, and at the complete disposal of the owner.

feedback   Information generated by and/or for decision-makers, executives or others to allow them to monitor and evaluate the level of performance attained with a view to ensuring that the results sought are achieved or improved upon. Such knowledge is intended to reinforce the motivation to attain desired objectives.

FIFO (first-in, first-out)   A method of accounting for inventory such that the prices of the earliest goods purchased including beginning inventory are assigned as the cost of goods consumed or sold in the period. This method results in ending inventory being valued in terms of recent costs. There is no necessary relationship with the physical flow of inventory.

filing of accounts   The delivery of accounts to the registrar of companies to comply with statutory requirements and for public inspection. Such accounts may be in full or modified form and must comply with the formats required by the Companies Act 1985.—See modified accounts.

final accounts   Term loosely used to indicate the profit and loss account and balance sheet prepared at year end. Strictly the balance sheet is not an account but comprises the balances remaining after those of the revenue and expense accounts have been transferred to the profit and loss account.

financial accounting   A subset of accounting which has as its primary aim the periodic reporting of the financial results and position of an entity.—Contrast management accounting.

financial expense   An expense incurred in managing finance including the raising of capital and the repayment of debt.

financial statements   Balance sheets, profit and loss accounts, statements of changes in financial position, notes and other statements, which collectively are intended to give a true and fair view of the state of affairs and profit or loss for the period under review.

finished goods   The output of production which is saleable.

first-in, first-out   See FIFO.

first-year depreciation   The term applied to the particular depreciation allowed for income tax purposes in the first year of use of a certain asset.—See accelerated capital allowances.

fiscal year   The Government's financial year. In the UK this year ends on the 5th April but many public bodies close accounts on the 31st March. Sometimes used to indicate the accounting period chosen by a particular organisation.

fixed assets   Those assets which it is intended to retain in the business beyond the period of current operations for the purpose of earning revenue and which are not intended for sale in the ordinary course of business.

fixed assets register   A record containing data of each significant fixed asset, including description, acquisition date, location, cost, depreciation, and disposition. It may be maintained in the form of a subsidiary ledger.

fixed budget   An estimate of expenditures and receipts at an assumed activity level. Normally authority to spend is restricted to the amount fixed in the budget.—Contrast flexible budget.

fixed capital
(a) A legalistic concept of capital viewing capital as property

33

intended to be retained within the business to produce income. Generally equivalent to non-current assets.—Contrast circulating capital.

(b) In the context of partnerships it refers to that portion of capital contributed by partners which is not intended to be withdrawn or varied, at least in the short-term.—Contrast current account; fluctuating capital.

fixed costs (expenses)   Expenditures or expenses that do not vary with the volume of activity, at least in the short run. Such costs become progressively smaller on a per unit basis as volume increases.—Contrast variable costs.

fixed manufacturing overhead applied   The fixed manufacturing overhead costs allocated to units produced during a period.—Compare overapplied overhead.

flexible budget   An estimate of expenditures and receipts for each of a number of activity levels and which can be readily related to changes in the level of activity. Also called variable budget.—Contrast fixed budget.

flow   The amount of a particular type of transaction occurring over a given period of time e.g. especially flows of receipts, payments, revenues, expenses.

fluctuating capital   The term used to describe the capital contributions of partners which, rather than remaining fixed, are varied from time to time by additional contributions, withdrawals, or the shares of partnership profits and losses.—Contrast fixed capital.

f.o.b.   Free on board some location, e.g. f.o.b. London. The invoice price includes delivery at seller's expense to that location, where title to the goods usually passes to the buyer.

footing   Adding a column of figures. Cross-footing (cross-adding) refers to adding a (horizontal) row of figures which are the totals of a number of columns.

footnote   See note.

f.o.r.   Free on rail at a location.—Compare f.o.b.

forced sale A sale not in the ordinary course of business.—See liquidation value.

foreign exchange gain or loss The gain or loss from holding monetary items, payable or receivable, in a foreign currency when exchange rates change (SSAP 20).

format The lay-out and order of presentation of accounts, especially as specified by the Companies Act 1985.

franchise The right, granted or sold, to use a name or to sell products or services.

freedom from bias A standard of reporting where accounting information has been impartially determined and presented. The accounting principle of objectivity is frequently defined as being a combination of the two accounting standards of freedom from bias and verifiability.

freehold Land held in absolute ownership.—Contrast leasehold.

full accounts The complete accounts as required for submission to members of a company or to the registrar of companies.— See abridged accounts; modified accounts.

full cost The cost of a unit of output which includes not only the variable costs of production but an appropriate proportion of fixed, indirect or overhead costs.—See absorption costing.

full costing See absorption costing.

full disclosure The presentation of all significant or material data in financial statements. Adequate disclosure is achieved when users of financial statements are provided with sufficient data to ensure that:
(a) financial statements are informative, reliable and not misleading;
(b) a basis exists for comparability with the financial statements of other periods and other entities.—Compare disclosure.

fund
(a) Noun – In the plural the whole or a specified portion of

the wealth or finance available to an entity. In the singular
a fund strictly implies a specified amount of wealth for
which the entity holds assets in a form which can ensure
that the amount is realisable to achieve the purpose of the
fund e.g. a pension fund and its investments.
(b) Verb – (i) To provide such wealth or finance.
  (ii) To record such provision in the entity's
      accounts.—See accumulated fund, statement of
      sources and application of funds.

funds derived from operations   The finance generated by an
entity from its trading activities. May be shown in a statement
of changes in financial position either as gross revenue less
expenses that involve the reduction of funds or as net profit
adjusted for items of income and expense that do not involve
the movement of funds e.g. especially by adding back the
change for depreciation of fixed assets financed in an earlier
period (SSAP 10).—See Statements of sources and application
of funds.

funds (flow) statement   See statement of sources and application
of funds.

fungible assets   Assets which individually are so similar as to
be indistinguishable and may be classed together.

future amount value   The amount to which a sum of money will
accumulate if invested at a particular interest rate for a given
period of time.

G

gain Increase in net assets arising other than from normal trading activity e.g. due to rise in the value of an asset not held for resale. Sometimes loosely used as a synonym for profit.—See holding gain.

gearing The relationship between the proprietors' capital and other long-term finance for an entity. This ratio affects the relative earning potential of the different parties providing finance.—See leverage.

gearing adjustment An adjustment required when converting historic costs to current costs to identify the re-stated profit attributable to shareholders allowing for the effect of the finance of operations by borrowing (SSAP 16).

general expenses A group of operating expenses each one of which is not material and does not fall under other recognised classes of operating expenses.

general journal A record of original entry in which is recorded all transactions not recorded in the special journals (e.g. cash receipts journal) maintained by the business.

general ledger The name for the ledger containing the accounts which appear in the financial statements. Also called the private ledger.

general price level accounting See current purchasing power accounting.

generally accepted accounting principles (G.A.A.P.) A title used in the United States to describe the conventions, rules, and procedures necessary to define accepted accounting practice at a particular time; includes both broad guidelines and relatively detailed practices and procedures. In the United States these are being codified in statements issued by the Financial Accounting Standards Board. In the UK the equivalent are the SSAPs.

going concern   The concept or assumption that a business will remain in operation indefinitely, i.e. it is not expected that operations will cease within the next accounting period. Also called continuity of operations (SSAP 2).

goodwill   An intangible asset of an entity which reflects its ability to earn more than a normal rate of return on its physical assets. Goodwill can arise from a number of causes. It is usually recognised in the accounts only when it is acquired through specific purchase. In this situation it is calculated as the excess of cost of the acquired entity over the current or fair market value of the net tangible asset acquired. Where not so recognised it is known as inherent goodwill.

gross margin (or profit)   Net sales minus cost of goods sold.

gross profit   See gross margin.

gross profit method   A method of estimating inventory at the end of a period, when a physical stocktake has not been made. If the gross margin on a firm's products and the mix of products remain relatively constant over time the established ratio of gross margin to sales may be used to calculate cost of goods sold and thus the ending inventory. For example: assume gross margin to sales is $33\frac{1}{3}$ per cent; sales for the month £12,000; opening inventory £5,000; purchases for the month £9,000; gross margin is $33\frac{1}{3}$ per cent of £12,000 viz. £4,000; cost of goods sold is £12,000 less £4,000 viz. £8,000; closing inventory is opening inventories plus purchases less cost of goods sold viz. £6,000.—Contrast retail inventory method.

gross sales   Sales at invoice prices, not reduced by discounts, allowances or returns.

group   A holding company together with its subsidiary company(ies) comprises a group.

group accounts   See consolidated financial statements.

guarantee (guaranty)   An undertaking to answer for payment of a debt or for the performance of an obligation by another person who is liable for payment or performance in the first instance. Frequently used as a synonym of warranty.

H

hire-purchase agreement   A contract for sale and purchase under which the consideration is payable by instalments over some specified time, but the title to the goods does not pass to the purchaser until the final instalment has been paid.— Contrast instalment sale agreement (SSAP 21).

historical cost price   See acquisition cost.

holding company   Is a company which by inference from the Companies Act 1985 exercises control over a subsidiary company. Also described as a parent company.—See subsidiary company.

holding gain or loss   The difference between the values at two different dates of an asset held between the dates concerned. May be realised by selling the asset or remain unrealised.

human resource accounting (H.R.A.)   The accounting for the impact of the knowledge, services, skills, loyalty, etc of employees on an entity's income-earning process and financial position.

I

IASC   An abbreviation for the International Accounting Standards Committee which represents accountancy bodies world-wide in attempting to establish standards especially for countries without or deficient in them.

ICMA   The abbreviation for the Institute of Cost and Management Accountants.

imprest fund   A fund to enable future expenses or outgoings to be met. The essential feature of an imprest system is that the original fund is maintained at its initial amount by periodic reimbursement of the exact amount of payments made from the fund. There is thus a limit set to the total amount of disbursements possible by the imprest holder.

improvement   An expenditure to extend the useful life of an asset or to improve its performance over and above that of the original asset. Such expenditure is capitalised as part of the asset.—Contrast repairs and maintenance.

income   The maximum value that could be withdrawn by the owners of an entity during a period without reducing the value of their stake in the entity below the level of the beginning of the period. Calculated in accounting as the excess of revenues and gains over expenses and losses for a period. Also called net income, net profit, profit.

income accounts   A term often used to describe *all* the accounts recording revenue *and* expense flows not just revenues. Also called nominal accounts or revenue accounts.

income and expenditure account   The financial statement of a non-profit making entity, similar to a profit and loss account, showing the expenses, revenues and resultant surplus or deficit.

income statement   The statement of revenues, expenses, gains and losses showing the results of an entity's operations in a period. Also called profit and loss account or revenue statement.—Contrast balance sheet.

income tax   An annual levy by the Government calculated on the income of an individual.

incomplete records   A description of recording methods which are not systematic and do not fulfil the requirements of double-entry recording.

incremental cost   The change in cost resulting from the production of an additional unit of output, etc. Also called marginal cost.

indirect costs   Costs of production not easily associated with the production of specific goods and services; overhead costs. May be allocated on some arbitrary basis to specific products or departments.

indorsement   A signing or instruction written on the back of a document, such as a bill of exchange or cheque. The indorsement usually results in the drawee's or payee's assigning the amount of the bill or cheque to another party. Also spelt endorsement.

information system   A system, formal or informal, for collecting, processing, and communicating data useful for the managerial functions of decision making, planning and control, and for financial reporting.

insolvency   The inability to pay debts as they fall due. Insolvency is a question of fact. A person could be described as insolvent and yet not have been adjudicated bankrupt. In contrast, a person who has been adjudicated bankrupt may eventually prove to be solvent, pay his debts in full, and apply for annulment of the adjudication.—See liquidation, winding up.

insolvent   The state of insolvency.

instalment   The partial payment of a debt or the partial collection of a receivable, i.e. an amount less than the whole sum due or receivable.

instalment sales agreement   A contract for sale under which the consideration is payable by instalments over some extended time period, and the title in the goods passes to the purchaser on delivery.—Contrast hire-purchase agreement.

intangible asset   A non-physical asset giving an entity probable future economic benefits arising from some exclusive, preferred, or protected position, e.g. franchises, goodwill, patents, or trademarks.

integrated accounts   Accounts so arranged as to provide the information required from a financial accounting system and incorporate cost accounts using the same prime data.

interest
  (a) The charge or cost for the use of money.
  (b) A right to, or a share in, the profits or assets of an entity, e.g. minority interest, interest in a partnership.

interim reports   Financial information about an entity relating to periods shorter than the financial year. Interim reports are usually less detailed than the (annual) financial statements and may be issued at irregular intervals.

internal audit   The continual examination of an entity's operations by designated staff employed by the entity. The purpose of the examination is to check the effectiveness of the systems and procedures employed and to report to management on failures or weaknesses noted.—Compare audit.

internal check   Those internal arrangements and procedures of an entity designed to provide automatic checks against improper practices, incomplete or inaccurate information, and deliberate embezzlement or fraud. Part of internal control.

internal control   The plan of organisation and all of the co-ordinate methods and measures adopted within a business to safeguard its assets, check the accuracy and reliability of its accounting data, promote operating efficiency, and encourage adherence to prescribed managerial policies.

internal rate of return   The rate of profit arising from an investment project determined by calculating the discount rate which would reduce future cash flows arising from it to its initial capital cost.

in transit   A reference to goods or cash which are in the process of being conveyed at balance date and are recorded as such.

inventory   Tangible property held:
  (a) for resale in the ordinary course of business; or
  (b) in the process of production for such sale; or
  (c) to be consumed in the production of goods or services for sale.
Also called stock, stock on hand, or stock-in-trade.—See stock valuation (SSAP 9)

investment   Property on other assets acquired or held in order to produce revenue.

investment appraisal   The process of evaluating the potential profitability or otherwise of investing funds.

investment centre   A part of an entity whose profitability is determined separately and related to the amount of investment in it.

invoice   A document recording the details of a sale or purchase transaction, including date, name of customer and vendor, quantities, prices, freight, and credit terms.—Contrast statement.

IPFA   The designatory letters for one who is a member of the Chartered Institute of Public Finance and Accountancy.

issued capital   The par value of shares allotted by a company.—Compare authorised capital.—Contrast issued shares; paid-up capital.

issued shares   The shares of a company that have been allotted to shareholders.—Compare authorised capital.—Contrast issued capital.

job cost sheet   A schedule showing inputs of materials, labour and expenses applicable to a particular order or job.

job cost system   See job order costing.

job order costing   A system, used in non-repetitive production situations, for accumulating the direct labour, material and expense incurred for each job or unit of output. An account is opened for each individual job to accumulate a record of these costs, with these accounts often forming a subsidiary ledger within the accounting system.—Contrast process costing.

joint cost   The total cost of producing by a single process two or more products which by their nature are not identifiable as individual products up to a certain stage of production, known as the split-off point. The concept also applies to any single operation resulting in two or more outputs.

joint product   One of two or more outputs from a single process. Joint products are not identifiable as individual products prior to a certain stage of production known as the split-off point.

joint venture   A one-off operation jointly mounted by two or more people or entities for which a separate set of accounts is kept.

journal   A book or record in which transactions are first recorded from prime data prior to further processing within the accounting system. Known as a book of original or prime entry and acts as a diary of transactions or events to be recorded in the ledger(s).

journal entry   A record in a book of prime entry, analysing a transaction in terms of debits and credits prior to posting to ledger accounts.

journal voucher A voucher evidencing a transaction, leading to, and frequently the authority for, an entry in the journal.

journalise To make an entry in a journal.

L

land   A fixed asset which is non-depreciable. In principle it should be accounted for separately from buildings situated on it, which are depreciable. (SSAP 12). Land held as an investment property is covered by SSAP 19.

last-in, first-out   See LIFO.

lease   A contract by which the owner of an asset (the lessor) permits another (the lessee) to use the asset for a stated time in return for payment at an agreed rate. The asset remains at all times the property of the lessor although sometimes the lessee is given an option to purchase the asset either during the currency of the lease or at its termination.

leasehold   A term used to describe land or property held other than in absolute ownership.—Contrast freehold.

leasehold improvements   Those expenditures, usually on buildings, made by the lessee to alter or improve leased property. Such improvements usually become the property of the lessor upon termination of the lease.

ledger   A systematic collection of individual accounts.—Compare general ledger, subsidiary ledger.

legal capital   See authorised capital.

lessee   See lease.

lessor   See lease.

leverage   The use of long-term debt in financing an entity. Financial leverage may be measured as the ratio of debt finance to equity finance or as:

$$\frac{\text{E.B.I.T.}}{\text{E.B.I.T.} - \text{interest.}}$$

—See gearing.

liabilities Liabilities are probable future sacrifices of economic
benefits stemming from present legal, equitable, or
constructive obligations of an entity to transfer assets or
provide services to other entities in the future as a result of
past transactions or events affecting the entity. The essential
characteristics of a liability are:
  (a) There is a legal, equitable or constructive duty to give
      satisfaction by the future transfer or use of assets at a
      specified or determinable date, on occurrence of a specified
      event, or on demand.
  (b) The entity has little or no discretion to avoid the future
      sacrifice.
  (c) The transaction or other event obligating the entity has
      already happened.

lien The right of a person to retain possession of the property
of another, or to have a charge over it, until such time as some
debt or obligation has been discharged.

life tenancy An interest in the income in an estate for the life
of the holder. On the death or other stipulated event
terminating the tenancy, the assets of the estate are disposed
of as directed in the will.—See also remainderman.

life tenant The holder of a life tenancy.

LIFO (last-in, first-out) A method of accounting for inventory
such that the prices of the latest purchased goods are assigned
as the cost of the goods consumed or sold in the period. This
method usually results in ending inventory being valued in
terms of other than recent costs. There is no necessary
relationship with the physical flow of inventory.

limited liability company A company the liability of whose
members is limited by shares or guarantee. In the case of the
former, liability is limited to the amounts unpaid on the shares,
in the case of the latter by the amount undertaken to be
contributed in the event of a winding up of a company.—See
private company, public company.

line department A department which is responsible for

attaining the firm's operational objectives such as production and sales.—Contrast staff department.

liquid assets   Cash and other assets readily convertible into cash. Also called quick assets.

liquidation   See winding up.

liquidation dividend   A payment to creditors on a winding up or bankruptcy when the creditors cannot be repaid in full or are repaid in instalments.—Contrast dividend.

liquidation value   The value placed upon an entity, usually a going concern, at a certain date, on the assumption that the entity ceases operations and is wound up on that date.

liquidator   The person appointed in terms of the Companies Act to wind up a company.

listed company (shares)   A public company whose shares are on the official list of a Stock Exchange and subject to its rules for dealing,—See quoted company, unlisted securities market.

lodgements not credited   See outstanding lodgements.

long-term (long lived) assets   See fixed assets.

loss   A decrease in service potentials available to an entity, other than withdrawals by owners, not matched by revenues or by inflows of other service potentials.—Contrast expense.

lower of cost or market rule   An accounting procedure providing for inventories to be carried at the lower of their historical cost and net realisable value thus leading to a cautious measure of income and asset valuation—See conservatism.

lower of cost or net realisable value   See lower of cost or market rule.

M

maintenance   See repairs and maintenance.

management accounting   A subset of accounting which has as its primary aim the reporting to management of information needed for decision making, planning and control.—Compare cost accounting.—Contrast financial accounting.

management by exception   A principle in management where attention is focused on performance that is significantly different from that expected or budgeted for.

management reports (accounts)   Reports or accounts produced for the use of management internally rather than for external publication.

manufacturing account   An account which records the labour, raw material and other factory costs of manufacturing a product or products in an accounting period. The proportion of the total cost for a period which relates to goods fully completed or finished is transferred to a finished goods stock account, or to the trading account if sold in the period as (part of) cost of goods sold. The balance represents the stock of work-in-progress or unfinished goods.

manufacturing costs   The costs of a product or activity, consisting of direct materials, direct labour, and factory overhead necessary to bring the product to completion. Selling and other non-factory costs are excluded.

margin
   (a) the difference between the selling price and the cost of an item.
   (b) The point at which consideration is given to increasing or decreasing an *extra* unit of production, expense, revenue, investment etc.

marginal cost   See incremental cost.

marginal costing   See direct costing.

market rate   The rate of interest applicable to current borrowings or investments as determined on the appropriate market for the security concerned.

market value   The value of an item as suggested by the current market prices of the item concerned, and likely to be obtained if disposing of the item.

marketable securities   Investments such as shares, stock and debentures in the Government, local authorities and companies that can readily be sold on the stock exchange, often held for conversion into cash as needed and treated as current assets.

mark-up percentage   The amount of gross profit expressed as a percentage usually of cost of goods sold or sales. For example a 25 per cent mark-up based on cost of goods sold is equivalent to 20 per cent on sales.

master budget   A comprehensive plan comprising all operating budgets. It usually includes projected financial statements for the budgeting period. Sometimes connotes the projected income statement only.

matching   An accounting procedure by which expenses incurred in earning particular revenues are offset against those revenues in the determination of periodic income.

material   Substantial or important enough to warrant or require specific identification in records or statements.

materiality   A doctrine which requires that material or significant features of an entity's financial position are disclosed, and permits, for the sake of convenience or to reduce cost, the breaking of the strict principles of accounting for trivial items e.g. where the cost of a hammer is treated as an expense not an asset, provided no serious distortion results.

maturity value   The amount to be paid or collected on the expiry of the term of a loan or investment.—Compare future value.—Contrast present value.

medium company   Similar to a small company but with higher levels of balance sheet assets, turnover and employees.—See small company.

memorandum of association   The formal document subscribed by those wishing to form a company and giving details of the company e.g. its name, objects and particulars of capital. The document and any subsequent alterations must conform to the requirements of the Companies Act 1985.

merger   The amalgamation of two or more businesses into a single economic entity.—Contrast takeover.

minority interest   The equity in a partly owned subsidiary which is not held by the parent company.

minute book   A record of business transacted at a meeting. Minute books are not part of the accounting system, but they are source documents providing supporting evidence and authority for some entries made in the accounting records.

modified accounts   Accounts for small and medium companies filed in an abbreviated or modified form from those required for larger companies. See abridged accounts; full accounts; publication of accounts.

monetary items   Assets and liabilities the amounts of which are fixed by contract or statute in terms of the monetary unit irrespective of changes in prices.

monetary record concept   The doctrine that accounting records are restricted to transactions which will take place and are measured in terms of money. Thus the value of goodwill etc. is not always reflected in the accounting records. Also known as money measurement concept.

monetary working capital adjustment   An adjustment made when converting historic cost to current cost accounts to allow for the difference in money required to finance credit transactions due to inflation.

mortgage   A charge over land given by the owner (borrower/mortgagor) to a lender (mortgagee) to secure repayment of a loan or to ensure satisfaction of a debt.

N

narration   A concise explanation following an entry in a general journal and quoting, where appropriate, the authority and evidence for the entry.

narrative form   A method of presentation of balance sheets and profit and loss accounts which displays both debit and credit items in a vertical form, with appropriate sub-totals, rather than in double-entry account form. Also called vertical form, statement form, report form.

net assets   Total assets minus total liabilities; proprietorship; owners' equity.

net book value   The difference between the original cost of an asset and its accumulated depreciation provision.

net current assets   Current assets minus current liabilities; working capital.

net income   See net profit.

net loss   Negative net income, or reduction of equity due to expenses exceeding revenues.

net present value   The difference between the present value of the net cash flows of a project or investment and the initial cash outlay.

net profit   The excess of all revenues and gains for a period over all expenses and losses of the period.

net realisable value (N.R.V.)   The estimated selling price in the ordinary course of business less costs of completion and less costs necessarily incurred in order to make the sale.—Compare exit value.

net realisable value accounting   The method of accounting in which exit values of assets are the basis for the preparation of financial statements.

net sales   Gross sales for a period less discounts, allowances, and returns.

net worth   See net assets.

nominal account   A revenue or expense account; an account which is closed off to profit and loss account at the end of an accounting period.

nominal interest rate   The rate of interest specified on a debt instrument.

non-adjusting events   Post-balance-date events which do not require alterations to the financial statements for the period just ended, but which should be disclosed in notes to those statements when their non-disclosure could affect the ability of the users of the statements to make proper evaluations and decisions.—Contrast adjusting events (SSAP 17).

non-monetary assets   Assets the amounts of which are not fixed by contract or statute in terms of a currency and may vary with changes in prices.

non-operating expenses/revenue   Those revenues and expenses arising from transactions incidental to the entity's main line(s) of business.

not-for-profit organisations   Institutions, societies and clubs whose primary object is the provision of services to members, and is not to make a profit. Any surpluses are accumulated within the organisation and used in the furtherance of the objects of the organisation. The term often includes public sector bodies.

notary public   A person, usually a solicitor, who attests deeds or writings primarily to make them authentic in another country.

note
   (a) Explanation of an item appearing in the financial statements. Also called footnote.
   (b) See promissory note.

O

objectivity   The concept that accountants should record and measure transactions impartially or with lack of personal bias.—See freedom from bias; verifiability.

obsolescence   The outdating of a product or process caused by improved alternatives becoming available that will be more cost-effective resulting in a decline in the market value of an asset. The decline in market value is unrelated to physical changes in the asset itself. Obsolescence is one of the factors which determines the economic life of a fixed asset, which in turn is one of the elements determining the basis of depreciation charged against the fixed asset.

off-balance sheet finance   The use of finance which does not require to be shown on the balance sheet since the asset provided by the finance is not owned by the entity e.g. an asset held under a leasing agreement. (SSAP 21).

opening entries   The journal entries necessary to record the initial assets, liabilities and owners' equity on the formation of an accounting entity.

operating budgets   Budgets prepared to assist in the planning and control of current activities, excluding those of a capital nature, e.g. sales, production, expense budgets.

operating cycle   See earnings cycle.

operating expenses   Expenses incurred in the ordinary activities of an entity. Normally includes only selling and distribution expenses, administration and management expenses, and financial expenses, thereby excluding cost of goods sold.

operating gain (or loss)   A gain or loss arising from trading etc. rather than simply from an increase or decrease in value due to holding goods or assets.—Contrast holding gain.

operating statements   The statements summarising in whole or in part, and in financial terms, the production and trading activities of an entity.

opportunity cost The present value of the income (or costs) that could be earned (or saved) from using an asset in its best alternative use to the one being considered. Opportunity cost is not ordinarily incorporated in formal accounting systems; for example a sole trader will not record the salary he might have earned in an alternative employment as a measure of his service (expense) to his business. Exit values may provide measures, or approximations, of opportunity costs.

option The legal right granted to a potential purchaser to buy something during a specified period at a specified price called the exercising price.

ordinary shares A class of shares which have no preferential rights as to either dividends out of profits or return of capital on a winding up.

organisation costs See preliminary expenses.

original cost See acquisition cost; historical cost price.

outlay See expenditure.

out-of-pocket cost (expense) A cost or expense whose amount is determined at short notice or by the particular requirements of the task e.g. taxi fares, hotel bills.

outstanding bankings or lodgements Deposits made to a bank account which have been recorded in the accounting system of the depositor but which have not yet appeared on the bank statement.

overapplied (overabsorbed) overhead The amount by which overhead applied to production exceeds the overhead costs incurred.—Contrast underapplied (underabsorbed) overhead.

overcapitalisation The existence of more capital funds than can be used to earn an adequate rate of return given the potential level of business activity.

overhead costs Costs that it is not practicable to trace and assign to the production or sale of identifiable goods and services.

Such costs are usually assigned at a predetermined rate thus leading to over/under absorption. Frequently limited to manufacturing overhead.

overhead rate   A standard or other predetermined rate at which overhead costs are applied to products or services. It is calculated as the amount of overhead costs for a period (estimated or actually incurred) divided by a measure of production activity such as direct labour-hours or machine-hours.

overtrading   Engaging in more business activity than available current resources can sustain without unduly increasing the risk of financial failure.

owners' equity   The interest of shareholders or other owners in the assets of an entity. At any time it is the cumulative net result of past transactions and other events and circumstances affecting the entity. In financial statements, owners' equity is shown as the recorded accountability of an entity to its owners. The characteristics of owners' equity are:
  (a) It is a general interest in an entity's assets, not a claim to specific assets.
  (b) Its amount is affected by the entity's operations and other events as well as by owners' investments in the entity and the entity's distributions to owners.
  (c) It is the interest that, perhaps in varying degrees, bears the ultimate risks of entity failure and reaps the ultimate rewards of entity success.

P

paid-up capital The amount paid by shareholders or recorded as paid on issued shares. It differs from the nominal value of shares issued by the amounts uncalled and called-up amounts in arrear.

par Face value or nominal value, e.g. if stock, shares or debentures are issued at par the amount payable equals the face or nominal value.—Compare discount; premium.

parent company See holding company

participating dividend A dividend paid to preference shareholders in addition to the normal preference dividends payable. The terms of issue must allow such further participation in earnings which would usually apply only after dividends on ordinary shares have reached a certain level.

participating preference shares Preference shares with rights to participating dividends or with rights to participate in surplus capital on the winding up of a company.

partnership The contractual relationship between two or more persons who agree to pool their efforts, knowledge and capital, or some of these with a view to earning profits to be divided between them. The governing Act is the Partnership Act 1890 and, with some exceptions, the maximum number of partners cannot exceed 20. Partners have unlimited liability for debts incurred by the partnership with the exception of a special category allowed by the Limited Partnerships Act of 1907.

partnership deed (or agreement) A formal contract between the members of a partnership which records agreed matters such as the duties and rights of the partners, the amounts to be invested and the procedure for sharing profits and losses. Where the deed or agreement is silent on some point, or if no deed or agreement exists, the provisions of the Partnership Act will apply. Note that a deed is in writing and under seal whereas an agreement may be in writing, verbal or implied.

pari passu   On an equal footing, or proportionately. A term frequently used with respect to share issues to indicate that the new shares being issued will rank equally in all respects with previously issued shares either immediately or at some specified time in the near future.

patent   An exclusive right granted by the Crown for manufacture, use and sale of a particular product. Since patents may be acquired by purchase or may be obtained directly from the Crown by the inventor, the cost may consist of the purchase price or of the expenditure leading to the application for the patent. Patents are granted for a period of 20 years.

P.A.Y.E.   'Pay as you earn'. A system of collecting income tax during the year in which the income is derived. For example, income tax is deducted from each payment of salary or wages before it is received by an employee. The deduction is made by the employer and the amount deducted is paid to the Inland Revenue Department. National insurance employee contributions are dealt with similarly to which are added an employer's contribution.

payee   The person or entity to whom a cash payment is made or who will receive the stated amount of money on a cheque.

percentage of completion method   The method of accounting for a contract partially completed at balance date, whereby a proportion of the estimated profit on contract is recognised in each accounting period as the contract activity progresses. (SSAP 9).

period cost (expense)   An expenditure charged as an expense of a given accounting period on the grounds that it is appropriate or convenient to regard it as benefiting that period alone. It is not assigned to units of output and cannot thus be treated as part of the value of stock carried forward to another period.—Contrast product cost.

period-end adjustments   Adjustments made to accounts at the end of an accounting period but before the preparation of the final accounts to ensure expenses and revenues are neither over nor under stated. The main adjustments are for accruals, prepayments, stock valuations and depreciation of fixed assets. The term may also include adjustments to rectify errors discovered.

periodic inventory method   See physical inventory method.

permanent differences   Differences between accounting profit before tax and that assessable for tax purposes by the Inland Revenue, due to the Inland Revenue's exclusion or inclusion of items of expense or revenue recognised or ignored in calculating accounting profit.—Contrast timing differences (Exposure draft 33).

perpetual inventory method   A method of accounting for inventories whereby both acquisitions and disposals of inventory are reflected in the inventory account at the time transactions occur. Perpetual inventory records will usually show both physical quantities and the money values of inventory that should be on hand at any time. Disposals and normal losses of inventory are transferred from the inventory account to the cost of goods sold account.—Contrast physical inventory method.

personal account   An account in which amounts owing to or by another entity or person are recorded.

petty cash fund   A special, relatively small, cash fund established for making minor cash disbursements in the operation of a business.—See imprest fund.

physical inventory method   A method of accounting whereby the acquisition of inventory is recorded in an expense account (purchases) and not in an inventory account. Periodically a physical count of inventory on hand is made and the cost or other value of this inventory is then computed and recorded in an inventory account. The cost of goods available for sale during the period may be determined by adding inventory on hand at the beginning of the period to the purchases during the period. The cost of goods sold is computed by subtracting the inventory at the end of the period from the cost of goods

available for sale. Also called periodic inventory method.—
Contrast perpetual inventory method.

plant register   See fixed assets register.

post-balance sheet events   Events which occur after the date of
a balance sheet but before the formal approval of the accounts
by a company's directors which are significant enough to
require adjustment or disclosure.—See adjusting events, non-
adjusting events. (SSAP 17).

post-closing trial balance   A trial balance taken after all nominal
accounts have been closed.

post-date   To date a document later than the date on which it
is actually completed and issued. A post-dated cheque is not
payable until the date shown on it.

posting   The formal transcribing of amounts from the journals
to the ledger(s) in an accounting system. The 'writing up' of
ledger accounts from subsidiary or prime entry records.

posting references   A series of abbreviations used to indicate in
the journal where an entry has been posted in the ledger, and
to indicate in the ledger the originating entry in the journal.

pre-closing trial balance   A trial balance prepared at the end of
the period before closing entries are posted.

pre-emptive right   The right of a shareholder to purchase a part
of any new share or convertible issue proportionate to his
existing holding in the company.

preference share   A class of share issued by a company which
receives priority over ordinary shares in the matter of dividend
payments and sometimes distribution of assets should the
company be wound up.

preferred creditors   Creditors entitled to payment before others
in the event of an entity being unable to pay off all due debts.

preliminary expenses   Expenses incurred in connection with the
formation and flotation of a company, e.g. stamp duties, legal
costs, costs of printing the memorandum, articles, prospectus,
etc. These expenses are of a capital nature, and are frequently

premium

shown initially as an intangible asset, to be written off at a
reasonably early date. Also called organisation costs.

premium The amount by which the price payable to a company
upon issue of stock, shares or debenture exceeds the face,
nominal or par value.

prepaid expenses See prepayments.

prepaid revenues See prepayments.

prepayments Expenditures made or revenues received in one
accounting period covering a term which extends beyond the
end of that period e.g. an insurance premium paid annually
in advance. To the extent that the expenditures or receipts
relate to the future period they should be carried forward in
the balance sheet. The term includes prepaid expenses (or
expenses prepaid), prepaid revenues (or income).

present value The value today of an amount to be paid or
received at some future date. Calculated as the future sum
discounted at an appropriate rate. Also called discounted
value.

price index A series of measurements indicating the
relationship between the weighted average price of a sample
of goods and services at various points in time and the
weighted average price of a similar sample of goods and
services at a common, or base, date.

prime cost The sum of direct materials, direct labour and other
direct costs attributable to a product.

prime data The initial or original data or documentary evidence
of an accounting transaction from which accounting records
are built up e.g. invoice, voucher, receipt etc.

principal
   (a) An amount of money which has been borrowed and on
       which interest is usually payable.
   (b) A person who employs an agent.

principles A term commonly used to describe the assumptions, conventions, and rules associated with the theory and procedures of accounting.

prior year adjustments   Entries made direct to retained earnings which do not affect the current year's profit or loss but arise from material changes of accounting policies or fundamental errors. (SSAP 6).

private ledger   See general ledger.

private (limited) company   A company which is not public, has at least two members and includes in its title the word 'limited' (or Ltd.) (See Companies Act 1985)—See limited liability company; public company.

process costing   A method of costing products where costs are computed on the basis of total costs divided by equivalent units of work performed. Often used in high-volume, similar products situations.—Contrast job order costing.

product cost   Any manufacturing cost that is assigned to units produced.—Contrast period cost.

profit   See income.

profit and loss account   The ledger account summarising the expenses, revenues, gains and losses of a given period and the resultant profit or loss as a balance. Often this account is abstracted as an income statement which also incorporates the profit and loss appropriation account.—See income statement.

profit and loss appropriation account   The account recording the profit or other funds available for distribution to owners or for retention in the business and the amounts so dealt with.—See retained earnings account.

profit centre   A part of an entity responsible for controlling both its expenses and revenues and evaluated by reference to its profitability.—See budget centre, investment centre.

promissory note   An unconditional written promise to pay a specified sum of money on demand or at a specified date. For accounting purposes promissory notes are treated the same as bills of exchange.—Compare bill of exchange.

property

property
   (a) An asset, owned, over which title is exercised.
   (b) The title to or rights of ownership in assets.

proprietorship   See owners' equity.

pro rata   Proportional(ly).

prorate   To allocate in proportion to some base.

prospectus   A formal printed document inviting the public to subscribe for or purchase any shares or debentures of a company.

provision   An amount entered into the accounts to ensure the expenses to be matched against revenues are fully allowed or provided for. Debits on appropriate expense accounts are matched by credits on provision accounts which appear on the balance sheet either as a contra to an asset account (e.g. provision for depreciation, provision for doubtful debts) or a liability (e.g. provision for maintenance). Provisions are of two main types:
   (a) those for depreciation, renewals or diminution in value of assets (re-valuation provisions)
   (b) those for known liabilities whose amount cannot be determined with complete accuracy (liability provisions).— Contrast reserve.

provision for depreciation   See provision.

proxy   A written authorisation given by one person to another so that the second person can act in place of the first person, e.g. attending and voting at shareholders' meetings; the person so authorised to act.

prudence   See conservatism.

public (limited) company   A limited liability company empowered to invite the general public to subscribe for its shares or other securities. It must have at least two members and to include the words 'public limited company' or plc in its name.

publication of accounts   Publication other than by delivery to the registrar of companies is deemed to exist by circulation or making them available for public inspection generally or to a class of members of the public e.g. customers or employees.— See abridged accounts, modified accounts.

purchase discount   A cash discount received by a purchaser.— Contrast trade discount.

purchase order   A document authorising a seller to supply goods.

purchases account   The account recording the acquisition of merchandise for resale by an entity. Depending upon the procedure adopted may also act as a stock account.

purchases returns and allowances (returns outwards)   See returns and allowances.

Q

qualifying capital interest   Equity share capital carrying the right to vote in all circumstances at general meetings.—See related company.

quantity discount   A reduction in purchase price granted because of the quantity purchased. Also known as bulk discount.

quick assets   Cash and bank balances, and assets which are readily convertible into cash, such as current marketable securities, and current receivables. Also called liquid assets.

quick ratio   The ratio of quick assets to current liabilities. An indicator of liquidity.

quoted company (shares)   Older term for listed company.—See listed company (shares).

R

rate of return The measure of profitability which relates earnings to capital employed. May be defined and measured in different ways depending upon the type(s) of capital involved.

ratio analysis The evaluation of financial statements by reference to ratios derived therefrom e.g. profit to capital employed, profit to sales etc.

raw materials All factory materials acquired for use in manufacturing a product.

real account An asset account other than a personal account. In North America the term refers to all balance sheet accounts (including personal accounts).

realisation The act of conversion into cash or a receivable e.g. by sale.

realisation concept The principle that revenue(s) and any related profit (or loss) should be accounted for as arising at the time possession in goods passes to a buyer, even though other times of recognition are possible e.g. on receipt of cash or signing a contract for supply.

realise To convert into cash or a receivable.—Contrast recognise.

receipts and payments account A financial statement prepared by a non-profit making entity which is essentially a summary of its cash (account) transactions for the period concerned.

receivables Amounts owed to an entity. They may be current (accounts receivable) or non-current (long-term receivables).

receiver A person appointed either by a court or by an individual under a power contained in a statute, or an instrument, to take possession of certain property for its protection, or to receive the rents, profits or income arising from certain property and to apply them as directed.

recognise To enter a transaction in the financial records of an entity.—Contrast realise.

recognition The act of entering a transaction in the financial records of an entity.—See revenue recognition.

redeemable shares Shares issued on the terms that they may be redeemed by the company at a later date, either by payment out of profits which would otherwise be available for dividends or out of the proceeds of a fresh issue of shares.—Contrast convertible notes.

redemption The process of paying off a mortgage or other debt or obligation.

related company Any body corporate in which an investing company holds on a long-term basis a qualifying capital interest, presumed to be 20 per cent or more of the body's nominal equity share capital, for the purpose of influencing or controlling the body so as to contribute to its own activities.—See qualifying interest.

relevant cost The cost pertinent to a decision.—Compare with incremental cost; opportunity cost.

relevant range That range in the volume of activity within which the assumptions made regarding cost behaviour patterns are valid.

remainderman The person entitled to a share of the assets of an estate after the cessation of the interests of the life tenant(s).—See life tenancy.

remittance A payment sent, or remitted, to someone or some entity.

repairs and maintenance The expenditures undertaken to preserve an asset's service potential for its economic life; these expenditures are treated as period expenses or product costs rather than capitalised.—Contrast improvements.

replacement cost See current replacement cost.

report form   See narrative form.

reserve
   (a) An amount of profits after tax, or other surpluses
       separately designated in shareholders' funds as being set
       aside for a particular or general purpose, or arising from
       a particular source. The profit or surplus set aside may be
       prohibited by statute from being distributed as a dividend,
       or the directors may intend that the amount is not available
       for distribution at least in the near future. The term also
       applies to the excess of a provision over that reasonably
       necessary for the purpose.
   (b) Sometimes all accumulated profits and surpluses are
       generally described as reserves.—Contrast provision.—See
       capital reserve; reserve fund; revenue reserve.

reserve capital   That portion of uncalled capital which the
   shareholders in a company have resolved shall not be capable
   of being called up except in the event and for the purposes
   of winding up.

reserve fund
   (a) A reserve represented by specific readily realisable and
       earmarked assets.
   (b) A reserve specifically labelled as a reserve fund by a
       requirement, for example, in the memorandum or articles
       of association of a company. In this case the reserve is
       unlikely to be represented by specific assets.—Compare
       provision; reserve; fund.

residual income   The net income available for distribution to
   ordinary shareholders, that is after allowing for preference
   share dividends.

residual equity   The interest of the ordinary shareholders or
   proprietors in the assets of the entity, as opposed to creditors,
   lenders, and other investors having a 'specific equity' in the
   assets.

residual value   The estimated or actual net realisable value of
   a depreciable fixed asset at the end of its economic life. Also
   called salvage value, scrap value.—Contrast book value.

retail inventory method   A method of estimating ending inventory by:
  (a) maintaining detailed records of all goods acquired and on hand at both retail and cost prices (and any changes in these);
  (b) calculating an average cost-to-retail percentage;
  (c) subtracting sales from the retail price of merchandise available for sale;
  (d) reducing the estimated inventory at retail prices to cost prices by applying the average cost-to-retail percentage.— Compare gross profit method.

retained earnings (account)   The account recording the addition to and distributions of profits and the balance of undistributed profits. Also called profit and loss appropriation account.

return on capital employed   The profit resulting from the use or investment of capital. Usually expressed as a percentage. The figures used in the calculation will depend upon how capital employed is defined e.g. equity capital, net assets etc.

returns and allowances   Reductions in the invoiced price of goods purchased or sold usually given because the goods have been returned to the seller, or, if kept by the purchaser, are not exactly what was ordered. The reductions are given by the seller issuing a credit note. The amounts of such adjustments are usually accumulated by the seller in a temporary revenue contra account called sales returns and allowances (returns inwards, and by the purchaser in an account called purchases returns and allowances (returns outwards).

revenue   The amount(s) earned by an entity from trading, rendering services or carrying out other activities during a given period.

revenue accounts   Accounts recording inflows closed at the end of the accounting period by transfer to the profit and loss account.

revenue expenditure   Expenditure which is expected to benefit only the current period and is treated as an expense in the profit and loss account of the period.—Contrast capital expenditure.

revenue received in advance   An item of revenue for which the cash has been received but the earnings process has not yet been completed, e.g. that part of rent received that relates to a future period. To the extent that the revenue relates to goods or services yet to be rendered it should be carried forward in the balance sheet. It may be shown included with accrued expenses or offset against prepaid expenses.—See prepayments.

revenue recognition   The adoption of criteria by which to decide which transactions shall be treated as identifying and measuring the revenue of an accounting period e.g. delivery of goods, receipts of cash etc.

revenue reserve   A reserve which is regarded as being available for distribution as a dividend through the profit and loss account.—Contrast capital reserve.—See reserve.

revenue statement   See income statement.

revenue transactions   Transactions affecting the (current) financial period recorded in expense or revenue accounts whose final balances are transferred to the profit and loss account.—Contrast capital transactions.

reversal entry   A bookkeeping technique whereby period-end adjustments which involve subsesquent receipts or payments are reversed as at the first day of the following accounting period. The net result of this procedure is to permit the routine recording of subsequent related receipts and payments without having to recognise the portions applicable to an earlier period.

right   The entitlement to subscribe to a new share or convertible issue.—See pre-emptive right.

ROCE   See return on capital employed.

S

sales (account)   The account recording revenue arising from selling goods or rendering services to a customer.

sales discount   A cash discount given by a seller.

sales returns and allowances (returns inwards)   See returns and allowances.

sales tax   The tax levied on the sale of goods either at the time of importation or on the manufacturer or wholesaler.— Contrast customs duty; excise duty.

salvage value   See residual value.

scrip   A document indicating possession of so many shares, bonds, etc. A share certificate.

scrip issue   See bonus issue

security
   (a) An item of value pledged by a debtor that money owing to a creditor will be paid. If the debtor fails to pay, the creditor may sell the item pledged and deduct the amount of the debt from the proceeds.
   (b) A financial instrument such as a debenture or Government Stock which offers formal security to the lender but loosely used to apply to a document that indicates ownership or indebtedness.

segmental accounts (reports)   The presentation of financial statements so as to distinguish between the different operations, markets or product lines of an entity e.g. showing trading results for different areas or classes of customer. Also known as disaggregated accounts.

selling and distribution expense   An expense of maintaining a sales organisation, of stimulating or making sales and of providing the physical means for distributing the firm's products to its customers.

semi-fixed (or semi-variable) cost   A cost which only partly varies in direct proportion with the level of output.

service department   See staff department.

service potential   Expected future benefits, e.g. in an asset.

share   A stated portion of the capital of a company recognising the amount of a holder's interest in the company.

share certificate   An instrument under the seal of the company which states that a person whose name appears on the certificate owns and is entitled to a specified number of shares in the company. Also called scrip.

share option   An option granted by a company to a potential purchaser allowing him to subscribe for shares in the company within a specified period of time at a prescribed price.

shareholders' funds (equity)   See owners' equity.

sight draft (bill)   A bill of exchange payable on demand (at sight).

sinking fund   A regular investment usually in interest-earning securities so that on conversion money will be available for the repayment of a liability or the purchase or replacement of an asset. Amounts equivalent to the investments are capitalised by periodic transfers from profits.

small company   One permitted by the Companies Act 1985 to file modified accounts. 'Small' is defined by reference to balance sheet total assets, turnover and average employees, criteria which may be subject to future amendment.—See medium company.

sole proprietorship (trader)   An unincorporated entity with a single owner.

source document   A document evidencing a business transaction or event.—See prime data.

source of funds   See statement of changes in financial position.

special journal   A journal recording only transactions of a particular nature that occur frequently, e.g. purchases, sales.

specific identification method   A method of accounting for inventories by identifying separately in the accounting records each unit purchased, sold and in inventory. Frequently used for items with large unit costs such as jewellery and cars.—Contrast FIFO; LIFO; weighted average inventory method.

split-off point   The point in the production process where goods with joint costs are physically separated.

S.S.A.P.   An abbreviation for *Statement of Standard Accounting Practice*.

stabilised accounting   See current purchasing power accounting.

stable monetary unit   A reference to the accepted practice in historical cost accounting of retaining in the records the monetary amounts of the original transactions without any adjustments for changes in the purchasing power of money.

staff department   A department which is responsible for advising and providing services to various operating departments. Also called service department.—Contrast line department.

standard cost   A predetermined cost established by specifying what amount and price an input of a product should be under planned conditions of working. Standard costs are used as a basis for identifying the variance of actual cost from standard, pricing, valuing inventories and other control and decision making purposes.

standard cost accounting   A method of accounting which uses standard costs in assigning and accumulating product costs, records actual costs and the differences between standards and actuals in variance accounts.

standards, accounting   See *Statements of Standard Accounting Practice*.

statement   A written summary of events during a period. A statement given to a debtor/creditor usually summarises one month's transactions and shows the balance upon which payment should be made.—See also financial statements.

statement form   See narrative form.

statement of affairs
  (a) A financial statement prepared for an entity, usually from incomplete records, akin to a balance sheet.
  (b) A similar statement drawn up to indicate the funds available for meeting debts, based upon expected realisable values, usually by a receiver in bankruptcy proceedings.

statement of assets and liabilities   See balance sheet.

statement of changes in financial position   A term sometimes used for a statement of sources and applications of funds.

statement of financial position   See balance sheet.

statement of retained earnings   See retained earnings (account).

statement of sources and applications (uses) of funds   A statement showing the resources provided (financing activities) and resources applied (investing activities) between two balance dates. SSAFs distinguish between revenue and capital transactions in increasing or decreasing available funds and their utilisation. They are required supplements to final accounts (SSAP 10).

Statements of Standard of Accounting Practice   These are statements promulgated by the Accounting Standards Committee, made up of representatives of the major British accountancy bodies, indicating the bases upon which financial statements are to be prepared for publication in order to disclose a true and fair view. Members of the professional bodies preparing, or auditing, financial statements must adhere to these standards or risk disciplinary action. Prior to their adoption exposure drafts (EDs) are normally issued for comment by interested parties. They are generally known as SSAPs with a number reference e.g. SSAP 2.

stock
  (a) Inventories. See stock valuation.
  (b) North American term for shares.
  (c) Fully paid shares which have been converted into (stock) units. Shares are numbered and are transferable only in

stock dividend

their entirety; stock units are not numbered and are transferable in fractional parts of their nominal value.

stock dividend   North American term for a bonus issue.

stock exchange   An institution which provides a regulated market for sellers and buyers of securities issued by the Government, companies and other corporate bodies.

stock-in-trade   See inventory.

stock on hand   See inventory.

stock valuation   The process of calculating the value of inventory or stock on hand. The method adopted depends upon the nature of the inventory ranging through raw materials, work in process, finished goods or goods for resale (SSAP 9).—See FIFO, gross profit method, LIFO, lower of cost or market rule, perpetual inventory method, physical inventory method, retail inventory method, specific identification method, standard cost. Note: these methods are not exhaustive or necessarily mutually exclusive.

subscribed capital   See issued capital.

subsidiary company   A company (S) is subsidiary of another (H) if that other (H) either:
(a) is a member of it and controls the composition of its board of directors; or
(b) holds more than half in nominal value of its issued equity share capital.
The term also applies to the relationship between a company (S) and another company (H) where S is a subsidiary of any company (S*) which is itself a subsidiary of that other (H).

subsidiary ledger   A ledger containing the individual accounts for a particular class of transactions; the total for the class is shown in a control account in the general ledger. For example, an accounts receivable subsidiary ledger contains details of transactions and balances relating to each customer, while the general ledger contains only aggregate figures in the control account.

substance over form   The concept that reality rather than simply legality should be reflected in financial statements e.g. the reporting of assets acquired on lease as if they were owned, so as to indicate more adequately the real position. (SSAP 21).

sundry creditors   See accounts payable.

sundry debtors   See accounts receivable.

sunk costs   Costs incurred in the past that are not affected by, nor affect, and hence are not relevant for, current decisions.

super profits   Profits in excess of the normal rate of return expected on capital employed for a given degree of risk. Used as a basis for calculating a payment for goodwill.

surrender value (of life insurance policy)   The amount that would be realised if the policy were surrendered to the insurance company and cancelled. It should not be confused with the face value of the policy to be paid in the event of death.

suspense account   A temporary account used to record individual debits or credits until such entries can be eliminated or transferred to an appropriate account as a result of fuller information e.g. identifying the correct account or discovery of an error.

T

'T' form   See account form.

take-over   The acquisition by one company of a controlling interest in another company through the purchase of shares from existing shareholders and/or from a new issue.—Contrast merger.

tangible asset   An asset having a concrete, physical form e.g. machinery, plant etc.

tax avoidance   See avoidance of tax.

tax evasion   See evasion of tax.

tax loss   The excess of allowable deductions over assessable income calculated according to the appropriate tax legislation.

taxable income   The excess of assessable income over allowable deductions calculated according to the appropriate tax legislation.

timing differences   Differences between accounting profit before tax and that assessable for tax purposes arising from the inclusion of items of income in periods different from those in which they are dealt with in the profit and loss account—Contrast permanent differences (Exposure draft 33).

trade creditors   Accounts payable arising from the purchase of goods or services.

trade debtors   Accounts receivable arising from the sale of goods or services.

trade discount   A discount from list price offered to all customers of a given type whose business involves dealing in the particular goods. Trade discount is deducted at the time of sale and only the net amount is recorded in the accounting records.—Contrast cash discount; quantity discount.

trading account   A ledger account or statement showing the gross profit arising from trading, i.e. sales less cost of goods sold; a component of the income statement.

trading on the equity   An older term for financial leverage.

transaction   Any event involving a change in the amount, sources, form or disposition of an entity's economic resources and thus recorded in its accounts. Not just events involving physical exchanges of cash, goods or services between an entity and an outside party.

transfer price   An internally determined price used to decide upon, or account for, the allocation or transfer of resources between departments of the same entity or members of a group. May be based on external market prices if available or appropriate.

trial balance   A listing of the accounts in the ledger and the summation of their respective debit and credit balances.

true and fair view   Companies Act requirement that financial statements should give a true and fair view of a company's position and that auditors should certify that such is the case. Compliance might require companies to provide more information than formally required by the Act or depart from a strict interpretation thereof.

turnover   The amount of revenue derived from the sale of goods or services. Equivalent to invoiced sales less returns and allowances.

U

unadjusted trial balance   A trial balance prepared before adjusting and closing entries are made at the end of the period.

unallotted shares   The total nominal value of authorised capital not yet allotted.

uncalled capital   The total amount of capital that as yet has not been called up by the directors on the shares which are currently issued.

underapplied (underabsorbed) overhead   The amount by which overhead applied to production falls short of the overhead costs incurred.—Contrast overapplied (overabsorbed) overhead.

undercapitalised   Inadequate capital funds to sustain a given level of trading.

undertrading   Trading insufficiently either to generate a profit or obtain an adequate rate of return.

underwriting   Agreeing, in return for a fee, to take up by way of subscription in a new company or new issue a certain number of shares if and so far as they are not applied for by the public. Underwriting of an issue is usually undertaken by a financial institution.

unexpired cost   The book value of an asset in the historical cost system.

uniformity   The use of the same accounting practices by more than one entity in the same or similar situations.—Contrast consistency.

unissued capital   See unallotted shares

unlisted securities market (USM)   A subset of stock exchange activities dealing in the securities of some companies whose shares are not listed.—See listed companies.

unrecovered cost   See unexpired cost.

use of funds   See application of funds.

V

value   The expected advantage or benefit from owning or using a given item, usually measured in monetary terms.—Contrast cost.

value added   The increase in value resulting from an extra stage of the productive process usually measured in terms of the costs of the extra inputs used and associated profit.

value added statement (report)   A statement presented so as to identify how the total amount of an entity's turnover has been contributed by, and distributed amongst, the different suppliers of resources e.g. suppliers, employees, lenders, shareholders etc.

value added tax (VAT)   A tax based upon the amount of value added. Thus, if VAT is at 15 per cent, a producer may buy raw materials costing £115 which includes £15 VAT. He sells, after incurring various costs, his product for £200 plus £30 VAT. He pays over to Customs and Excise £30 minus £15, thus recovering the VAT paid on raw materials, the raw materials producer pays over £15, whilst the final consumer bears the full £30 calculated upon value added at various stages.

value for money audit   An audit to assess the efficiency of management rather than the mere compliance with legal or internal control procedures concerned primarily with the accuracy and correctness of financial procedures.

variable budget   See flexible budget.

variable costing   See direct costing.

variable costs   Those costs which respond proportionately to changes in the volume of activity within the relevant range. Variable costs are not necessarily assigned as direct costs of units of output.

variance   The difference between the actual and standard or planned inputs or outputs, e.g. the difference between budgeted and actual expenditures.—See standard cost.

VAT   See value added tax.

verifiability   An attribute of information such that qualified individuals working independently of one another will develop essentially similar measures or conclusions from an examination of the same evidence. Less strictly, the ability to obtain evidence for an accounting entry or measure.

vertical form   See narrative form.

voucher
  (a) A document that serves to recognise a liability and initiates payment
  (b) Sometimes used to refer to the written evidence documenting an accounting entry in a journal.

W

warranty   An undertaking by a vendor that goods sold are fit for use or fulfil specified conditions; a stipulation in a contract of sale the breach of which may give rise to a claim for damages but not to a right to reject the goods and treat the contract as repudiated. When warranties are given, the appropriate accounting treatment is to provide in the accounts for the estimated cost of meeting the warranties. The provision is an expense of the period in which the sale is made.

wasting assets   Assets which physically become exhausted e.g. quarries, coal mines etc.

way-bill   A document setting out details of passengers carried or of goods sent with a public carrier.—Contrast bill of lading; consignment note.

weighted average inventory method   A method of inventory valuation which takes into account the varying prices and quantities of goods purchased. May be calculated as either:

(a) the weighted average cost of all goods available in a period; or

(b) more usually as a weighted moving average cost recalculated at the time each new shipment is received.

winding up   The process by which the business activities of a company are brought to an end. The process is akin to the administration of a deceased estate and to bankruptcy, however a company must be wound up in accordance with the Companies Act. Liquidation is sometimes synonymous with winding up.—Compare dissolution.

window dressing   The practice(s) adopted in order to ensure financial statements reflect the most favourable position e.g. delaying purchase of assets to show more cash in the balance sheet than would otherwise be the case.

work in process   See work in progress.

work in progress   Products, services or contracts partially completed at a specified time, usually balance date. Usually classified as inventory in the balance sheet. Also called work in process.

work sheet   An informal accounting document which facilitates the preparation of financial statements without making period-end adjustments and closing entries in the accounting records. The formal entries are made in the records at a later date.

working capital   A measure of the long-term investment required to finance the day-to-day operations at a given level of activity; current assets minus current liabilities.

write down (up)   A revaluation of an asset downwards (up-wards).—Contrast write off.

write off   To reduce or eliminate the recorded value of an asset in the accounts by treating it as an expense or loss of investment e.g. an asset's depreciation or destruction by fire.—See expense.